Remembering
The University of
Michigan

Michael Chmura and Christina M. Consolino

TURNER

PUBLISHING COMPANY

All-American and All-Big Ten player Tom Harmon (no. 98) in Michigan's 40–0 victory over Ohio State in 1940. During this year, he was awarded the Big Ten Most Valuable Player and became Michigan's first Heisman Trophy winner. Harmon was considered one of the greatest halfbacks of his time. Two years later, he joined the U.S. war effort as a military pilot and received a Silver Star and Purple Heart during his service in China.

Remembering
The University of
Michigan

Turner Publishing Company
4507 Charlotte Avenue • Suite 100
Nashville, Tennessee 37209
(615) 255-2665

Remembering the University of Michigan

www.turnerpublishing.com

Library of Congress Control Number: 2010924317

ISBN: 978-1-59652-660-0

Printed in the United States of America

ISBN: 978-1-68336-893-9 (pbk)

10 11 12 13 14 15 16—0 9 8 7 6 5 4 3 2 1

CONTENTS

The University of Michigan Marching Band forms a Block M on the field of Michigan Stadium in 1964, under the direction of William D. Revelli, one of America's most influential college band directors. The Marching Band began in the late 1800s as a grass roots student effort and first appeared on the football field in 1898. In 1983, it was the first recipient of the Louis Sudler National Intercollegiate Marching Band Trophy, which recognizes excellence in marching bands.

ACKNOWLEDGMENTS

This volume, *Remembering the University of Michigan,* would not have been possible without assistance from the Bentley Historical Library, University of Michigan. It is with great thanks that we acknowledge the valuable contributions of its dedicated staff.

The photographs within this volume were chosen from the following collections of the Bentley Historical Library and are used by permission:

University of Michigan Board in Control of Intercollegiate Athletics, UM Alumni Association, the UM Athletic Department, the UM Department of Physical Education for Women, UM News and Information Services, Ivory Photo, UM Photographic Vertical File, Ann Arbor Garden Club (HS 1823), James B. Angell papers (HS 1824), the papers of William Revelli, and the papers of Fielding Yost

We would also like to thank the following individuals for invaluable suggestions and feedback:

Dave Chmura

Tim Meade

Traci Parker

Mary Beth Sheehan

The Michigan Theater is considered a landmark. In this photograph from 1948, a line of people wait to view the premiere of *It Happens Every Spring*. The theater opened in January 1928 and was a showplace for both live entertainment and movies in its two theaters.

PREFACE

The photographs on these pages capture the story of how the University of Michigan grew after moving from Detroit to Ann Arbor in 1837. Over the course of 170 years, the school expanded from seven students and two professors to become an internationally acclaimed institution, creating magnificent architecture, renowned hospitals, and respected research facilities where empty meadows once stood. A polio vaccine, radio-wave technology, and continuing research into peaceful, productive uses for nuclear energy are only part of the University of Michigan's proud history.

The university is frequently credited with popularizing football west of the Alleghenies. Its Wolverines and their famed coaches rushed and passed their way into the history books. One former gridiron star became a movie actor. Another rose to the office of President of the United States. Other sports created their own legends, such as hockey star Robert White and aquatic gold-medal winner Maxine "Micki" King.

The remarkable black-and-white photographs within this book were carefully selected from Bentley Historical Library's extensive collections. With the exception of cropping where necessary and touching up imperfections that have accrued with the passage of time, no changes have been made. The focus and clarity of many images is limited to the technology of the day and the skill of the photographer who captured them. We hope they will help readers to fondly recall memories of crossing the Diag with sunlight streaming through trees, of cheering another Wolverine athletic victory, and of the instructors, classes, and students that made a difference in their lives.

Originally built in 1841 and referred to as the University Building, Mason Hall was the home of the Literary Department (later College of Literature, Science, and the Arts), the first department of the university. This picture is from around 1850, after it had been officially named Mason Hall, in honor of Michigan's first governor, Stevens T. Mason. The building provided study space and dormitories for the students, as well as classrooms for instruction.

BUILDING A GREAT UNIVERSITY

(1870s–1899)

Two students lounge on a sunny day near the northwestern corner of campus around 1873. The boulder against which they rest was known as the "Pudding Stone," the "Big Stone," or the "Senior's Pet Pebble," and was placed on campus February 24, 1862, by the Class of 1862. Throughout the years, the boulder has had many homes, but in 2005 it came to rest outside the C. C. Little building, the current home of the Geology Department.

A view from the northwest corner of campus around 1873. People in horse-drawn carriages ride along State Street in front of the Law Building and University Hall. Shown behind the fence is the Class of 1862 memorial boulder.

Students enjoyed walking to class under the trees, as shown in a photograph from 1873 or 1874. The walk extended from the northwest corner, past the Law Building and University Hall towards South University.

Built in 1871 by E. S. Jenison of Chicago, University Hall is shown with its original dome in 1873. The building was constructed to connect Mason Hall and South College, thus forming a showpiece building for the University of Michigan. It provided a chapel, an auditorium, lecture rooms, and office space under a dome that rose 140 feet above the ground.

In 1855, Dr. Henry Tappan cited the need for a chemical laboratory, which was built in 1856 under the direction of architect A. J. Jordan, the first of its kind at a state university. The building was enlarged multiple times between 1861 and 1868. The photograph shown here depicts the Chemical Laboratory in 1874, after its fourth wing was added. Further additions took place in 1880, 1889, and 1901.

Sophomores sit in the grass outside University Hall in 1877. The building drew great criticism because of the size and design of the large dome, as well as the turrets—known as "pepper boxes"—at the base of the dome. University Hall underwent changes during Christmas break, 1896, with the replacement of the original dome with a smaller and less-expensive iron one. The building was demolished in 1950.

The University of Michigan Law School has historically attracted many students. Some of them are shown here studying in the library of the Law Building, which was originally housed in Old Haven Hall. The Law Library occupied the second floor of the south wing. This photograph was taken in 1877.

A university boat is led by a ladies' crew team on the Huron River around 1878-79.

The Law Building as it stood on the northwest corner of the campus, photographed between 1863 and 1893. The Regents of the university renamed the building Haven Hall, in honor of Erastus O. Haven, president of the university from 1863 to 1869. Old Haven Hall was a home not only for the Law Department (later the Law School), but also the University Chapel (until 1873) and the General Library (until 1883).

The first University of Michigan football team finished the season with a record of one win and one tie. Its captain, David N. DeTar, is shown in the back row, third from the left, in this 1879 photograph. The 1879 season was the founding season for varsity football at the university. The teams functioned without coaches until 1891.

By 1850, diagonal paths across the campus had emerged, created by students and faculty walking from corner to corner. These paths were covered with boardwalks; the major path became known as the Diag. This photograph shows a view from the old fence posts at the northwest corner of the campus in 1879. The many trees shown here were most likely planted around 1850, to lend a more formal air to the interior of the campus.

View from the west side (State Street) of University Hall as seen in 1880, after remodeling in 1879. During the renovation, two corner turrets and the "pepper boxes" at the corners of the roof were removed. This photograph clearly highlights the original dome, standing 140 feet above the ground, which was not removed until 1896.

The first Engineering Building at the University of Michigan was known as the Scientific Blacksmith Shop. Shown here in 1882, the building was the first fireproof building constructed on campus and contained a foundry, a forge, and woodworking and machine tool shops. The building was eventually sold and moved for use as a private residence at North University and Observatory.

Interest in music began to rise in the late 1870s and 1880s. The Chequamegon Band and Orchestra, shown in 1888, was a part of the growing music trend and often played at parties and concerts.

John Jacob Abel (seated) and his assistant, Archibald Muirhead, in the Pharmacology Laboratory around 1891. Abel received his Ph.B. from the university in 1883, and founded and chaired the first Department of Pharmacology in the United States at the University of Michigan in 1891. He is known for being one of the first to isolate epinephrine (adrenaline) as well as insulin in crystalline form and is often referred to as the Father of American Pharmacology.

The need for a new University of Michigan hospital became apparent by the end of the 1880s, and one was erected in 1891. It consisted of the two buildings shown here in the 1890s, the Homeopathic Department of Medicine (left) and the Allopathic Medical School (right).

Constructed between 1848 and 1850, the original Medical Building was the university's first medical building. It underwent several additions and served as the medical school's primary instructional building, providing space for lectures, recitations, anatomical dissections, laboratories, and faculty offices until 1903. Apparent in the photograph, taken between 1870 and 1903, is the Greek Revival portico on the eastern side of the building.

Workers are shown constructing Newberry Hall between 1888 and 1891, directly across State Street from University Hall. Nearly half of the building's cost was covered by a gift of Helen H. Newberry. To recognize this support, the building was named in honor of her husband, John S. Newberry, Class of 1847. Newberry Hall was headquarters for the Students' Christian Association. The building is constructed of native fieldstone in the Romanesque style of the period.

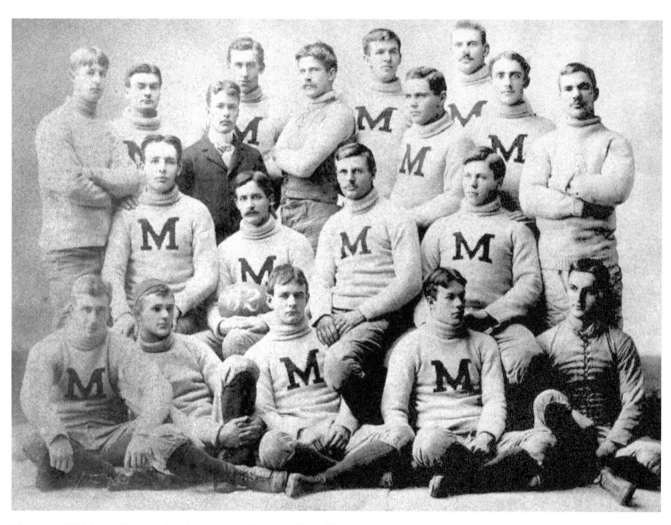

The 1891 UM football team played to an overall record of 4-5. The team captain was James Van Inwagen (2nd from left, middle row), and the coach was Frank Crawford (second from left, bottom row). The gentleman in the suit is the manager, Royal T. Farrand. Crawford and Van Inwagen were coach and captain for one year.

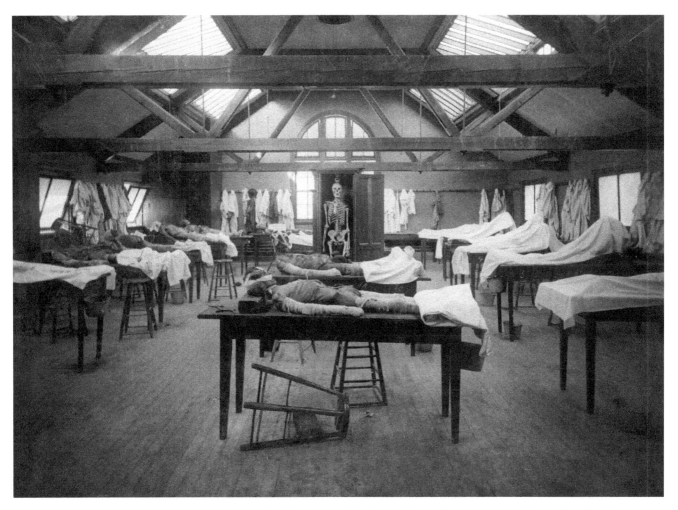

In 1889, a new building to house the Anatomical Laboratory was built in order to alleviate overcrowding within the department. The main laboratory, shown as it appeared in 1893, was on the second floor of the building. Skylights and small windows provided illumination. In this room, male medical students dissected cadavers.

The Anatomical Laboratory Building was also home to a dissecting room for women, shown here on the first floor of the building, around 1893. Although the first woman graduated with a medical degree in 1871, the women had separate dissection rooms from the men until 1908.

A view from State Street as it appeared in the late nineteenth century. To the far right is University Hall with its original dome intact. In the center sits the Law Building, after construction of an addition with a tower.

Alice Hamilton (third row, eighth from left) and other medical school students received instruction on surgery and anatomy in amphitheaters, much like this one photographed in 1893. After receiving her medical degree from the university and undertaking graduate studies, Hamilton conducted surveys on industrially related diseases and famously investigated the effects of manufacturing explosives on those that worked with them. She is regarded as a founder of industrial toxicology.

An organic chemistry lecture, probably in the original Chemistry Building, around 1893.

Between 1863 and 1923 the Law Building was home to the Law School, although expanding enrollments throughout the time made two considerable remodelings necessary. In 1893, more class and lecture rooms were added, as well as a tower on the northwestern corner of the building. The building is shown here, with the Class of 1862 memorial boulder in the foreground, between 1893 and 1897.

Forrest Hall, James Baird, Bert Carr, and James Hooper (left to right) were all a part of the 1895 University of Michigan football team. Coached by William McCauley, their overall record was 8-1. Their only loss that year was to Harvard University.

The Allopathic Hospital (also called University Hospital) on Catherine Street, as seen in 1897. The hospital opened in 1891 and the building converted to the Surgical Ward in 1900. The building would ultimately become a variety of wards and centers, including the East Convalescent Ward, the Rapid Treatment Center, and the Institute for Social Research. The structure was demolished in 1965.

Louis Elbel is shown in his room at Professor Alexander Winchell's octagonal house at the end of the nineteenth century. Elbel is known for composing the march famously titled "The Victors," after the 1898 football team won its first conference championship against their toughest opponent, the Chicago Maroons. Elbel, reportedly impressed and elated, determined that the university did not have the "right" celebratory song and composed the new march on his return train to Ann Arbor.

An 1899 photograph shows University of Michigan Law School students (the "Laws") celebrating their football win over the students from the Literary College (the "Lits"). A fierce rivalry between the two groups of students stemmed from an 1894 decision of the Lits to wear academic gowns at their commencement services. The Laws opposed the idea, and thus a competition between the two groups was born.

Acquired in 1870 as a class gift, a statue of Ben Franklin stood on the west side of State Street prior to 1899. While the class thought they had purchased a bronze statue, it was actually made of pewter, which could not withstand the abuse bestowed on it by students. It was removed from the campus after Franklin's arm fell off due to expansion of concrete that had been used to fill the hollow sculpture.

A baseball game at Regents Field (originally called the Athletic Field) in 1900. The field was laid out such that both baseball and football would be accommodated by one venue. A covered grandstand that seated approximately eight hundred can be seen on the left, the north end of the field. The original grandstand, which only seated four hundred, burned in 1895.

Growth in the Early Twentieth Century

(1900–1919)

Senior Swing Out was a tradition that marked the anniversary of the first wearing of the cap and gown in 1894. During this event at the beginning of the week of commencement, students would come together, sing Michigan songs, and parade to the auditorium to listen to speeches, usually given by the university president.

Charles Archibald "Archie" Hahn won the 220-yard dash against Chicago at Regents Field in 1903. Hahn studied law at the university, while also competing in track competitions. He won the 1903 Amateur Athletic Union title, and went on to compete in the 1904 St. Louis Olympic Games, where he won three gold medals. Having been born in Wisconsin, Hahn's nickname was the "Milwaukee Meteor."

Snow blankets the area around University Hall between 1898 and 1924. Note that the original, large dome has been replaced with a smaller, iron one, and the balustrades have been removed. The new roof and dome were designed by the Detroit architectural firm of Spice and Rohn.

Women did not participate in intercollegiate competition until 1920, but still enjoyed competitive pursuits through such avenues as field hockey, as shown in 1905. Teams consisted of women from the same class, the same sorority, or the same dormitory. Women's field hockey did not become a varsity sport until 1973.

The exterior view of the Anatomical Laboratory as it appeared between 1889 and 1903. Because demand for quality anatomy facilities grew, the Regents authorized construction of one of the first buildings dedicated to the study of anatomy in the country. Gordon W. Lloyd of Detroit was the architect. Erected on the eastern side of the central campus, south of the Old Medical Building, it was completed in 1889.

A crowd gathers in front of Ferry Field on Hoover Street between 1906 and 1909. Shown are the brick wall that surrounded three sides of the field, the front gate, and the ticket offices. During this time, a new gridiron was constructed, and Ferry Field was used solely for football games. It was later converted to an outdoor track-and-field facility.

The original General Library, photographed between 1897 and 1918, was both library and art gallery. Built in 1883, stacks were added to the south in 1898. The library was considered a campus landmark, due to its twin towers, semi-circular reading room of red brick, and the art gallery on the second floor. The 1883 portion of the building was taken down in 1918, when a new library was built, incorporating the old stacks.

The annual rush between freshman and sophomores, as photographed between 1907 and 1918. Called Push Ball, male students from each class lined up facing each other on the field, with space in between. Each class then tried to maneuver a large ball to the other side of the field without being crushed. The sport was deemed too dangerous and was eventually replaced by tug-of-war.

The cornerstone of Alumni Memorial Hall was laid in June 1908 by Judge Claudius B. Grant. Dedicated to members of the university who had served their country in the armed forces, the idea for the building actually dates back to 1864, but it wasn't until 1904 that the southwest corner of campus was secured for the site. Originally, it housed the university's art collection, moved from the library, but it has been put to many uses over the years.

The construction of the Waterman Gymnasium for men brought about the campaign to build a gymnasium for women. The building, designed by E. W. Arnold, was constructed in 1895-96, and named Barbour Gymnasium in 1898 in honor of Levi Barbour, who donated land that was ultimately sold to help finance construction. Both gymnasiums are shown here between 1902 and 1916 (Barbour on left, Waterman on right).

In 1912, football games were still played at Ferry Field. The kickoff of the last home game of that season, November 16, is shown here. The Wolverines, under Coach Fielding Yost, defeated Cornell, 20–7. As always with Michigan games, fans packed the stadium to capacity.

A view of the campus and the Diag as seen from the Engineering building located at the southeast corner, between 1908 and 1918. On the left stand the Engineering shops, while on the right is the Boiler House. Directly behind the Boiler House in this view is the Chemistry Lab.

The Barbour Gymnasium was central to all women's activities, such as this 1910 basketball game. In addition to the gym, the first floor also housed offices for the Department of Physical Education for Women and the Dean of Women. Besides physical education activities, Barbour Gymnasium was regularly used for large social occasions.

Senior women in cap and gown at Lantern Night in 1911. Lantern Night was an annual tradition and part of commencement activities. On that night, senior women passed lanterns to junior women, symbolizing the passing of another academic year.

In the early 1900s, the junior class began hosting a dance known as the Junior Hop, or J-Hop. Often celebrated in Waterman Gymnasium, J-Hops began at a local hotel called Gregory House in 1872. These students form the block M at the J-Hop in 1912.

The original General Library under a blanket of snow, photographed from the north, which allows a view of the circular reading room with the art gallery on top. Students using the reading room were separated by gender. At this time, the library's bookstack capacity was 200,000 volumes. Aside from the fireproof bookstacks, the building was declared a fire hazard in 1915, the year after this picture was taken.

Former University President James Burrill Angell's funeral procession on April 3, 1916. The procession made its way up State Street (where this photo was taken) to North University, Washtenaw, and Geddes avenues. "Prexy Angell," as he was affectionately known, served the university for 38 years and has the distinction of being Michigan's longest-serving president.

Due to space constrictions on campus, further expansions of the old General Library were impossible. The decision was made to build a new library on the same site, retaining the old stacks. Two stacks were built at right angles to the old ones, as shown in this photograph from 1917. Later, in 1918, what remained of the old library was demolished, and construction of the new General Library began.

Fielding "Hurry Up" Yost, head football coach 1901-23 and 1925-26, buys a Liberty Bond in 1917. Under Yost, the Wolverines won ten Big Ten championships. Twenty of his players became All-Americans. In 1901–1905, his teams outscored opponents 2,821 to 42. His 16-3-1 record against rival Ohio State is the best among UM football coaches. The College Football Hall of Fame describes his "Point-a-Minute" teams as the most devastating in the sport's history.

A group of students marches up Hoover Street in 1918. Ann Arbor and the University of Michigan supported President Wilson and World War I. Students became involved in naval militia units, ROTC, and the armed forces. In April 1918, the War Department asked the university to train non-college draftees as machinists, gunsmiths, blacksmiths, mechanics, and carpenters.

During World War I, divisions of the Naval Reserves were housed in Waterman Gymnasium. In this picture from 1918, a group of university students is being sworn into the Navy. Other buildings and sites were also put to use for the war effort, including Ferry Field and the Michigan Union.

A Rope Contest on Ferry Field on May 18, 1918, was part of the students' annual Spring Games.

The winner of the 1918 Spring Games was the Class of 1921, who were just freshmen at the time.

Students dance around a maypole in the spring of 1910. The maypole dance was the finale of what was commonly known as the Freshman Pageant, a part of commencement activities that occurred before the Lantern Night procession.

The Engineering shops were originally built next to the first engineering building, the Scientific Blacksmith Shop. An expansion in 1887 removed the Scientific Blacksmith Shop and left the building with a central tower, a one-story forge and foundry shop, and a west wing. In 1918, a clock and chimes were removed from the old General Library and added to the building, as shown in this photograph.

The Spring Games of 1918 included the Freshman-Sophomore Tug-of-War across the Huron River. First held in 1890, the tug-of-war could be seen on campus through the 1970s and often drew crowds as large as seven thousand. Only two rules existed: (1) Standing in more than two feet of water was not allowed; (2) The first team to pull the other into the drink was the winner.

A view from the Michigan Union tower, facing northeast in 1919, shows from left to right the Law Building, University Hall, University Museum, and Alumni Memorial Hall. Behind University Museum is the New General Library.

Originally the southeastern Professor's House, after renovations this building housed the School of Dentistry until 1892, when the building was renovated and enlarged to be used by the School of Engineering. The School of Engineering occupied the Old Engineering Building, shown here in 1919, from 1892 until 1922.

On a snowy day in 1921, a photographer took a picture of the view one would see if walking toward the West Engineering Building. The path, leading from the Diag to East University, crossed under the arch of the building. The arch is properly known as the Denison Archway but became commonly referred to as the Engin Arch.

FROM CAMPUS EXPANSION TO THE GREAT DEPRESSION

(1920–1939)

The Martha Cook Building in 1921. Constructed in 1915 as a residence for women, it was the result of a donation from William Wilson Cook in honor of his mother, Martha Walford Cook. The building was designed by New York architects York and Sawyer and is located on the block between South University and Tappan avenues. The grounds around the building included an expansive garden and tennis court.

Women play golf in 1922, one of few sports offered to them during this time. It was not recognized as a varsity sport until 1976.

Ice hockey became a varsity sport for men during the 1922-23 season. Coach Joe Barss, standing at right, is shown with his inaugural team. A University of Michigan Medical School graduate and World War I veteran, he led his team to a 26-21-4 record over five seasons. The captain of the 1922-23 team, Kyle MacDuff, is in the back row, fourth from the left.

A southwest aerial view of the campus around 1923. In the foreground is Ferry Field, with an at-capacity crowd watching a football game's halftime show. The dome of University Hall and the tower of the University Museum are in the background. The white building at the top of the photograph is University (Old Main) Hospital.

A photograph taken from East University Avenue between 1922 and 1925 shows the West Engineering Building, designed by Mason and Kahn of Detroit and completed in 1904. In 1909-10, an extension was added to the east wing over the Naval Tank. The building was known as the New Engineering Building, but was renamed West Engineering when a new structure built across East University was named East Engineering.

The New General Library was constructed between 1916 and 1920 on the same site as the Old General Library. Four stories tall and designed by Albert Kahn, the building was much like libraries found at Harvard and University of California. The only surviving structures from the old building were the bookstacks. The North face of the library is shown here in a photograph that dates from 1920 to 1925.

The Yost Field House dedication in 1923. Constructed that same year, the field house was designed to be a home for football, baseball, basketball, and track events. It was named after the great football coach, Fielding H. Yost. The band in this photo is the Marine Band, which attended the festivities along with fifteen hundred Marines and Secretary of the Navy Edwin Denby.

A northern view of Yost Field House. It was constructed on State Street, on the east side of Ferry Field, in Italian Romanesque style. The massive structure was built with roof trusses that could support not only the roof, but also four balconies. The large size of the field house benefited the football, baseball, and track teams, which were able to practice even in the winter and early spring.

The football teams play against the Quantico Marines in this photograph from November 10, 1923. At halftime, the Marine Marching Band formed a familiar "M" with the hopes of inspiring their team to victory. The Wolverines ended up winning the game, 26–6, in front of a crowd of 40,000 at Ferry Field.

The front face of the Michigan Union around 1923. The building, finished in 1919, was considered massive compared with clubhouses used by students at other universities. The interior was also built on a large scale and included a large lobby on the first floor, several dining rooms with well-equipped kitchens, 60 sleeping rooms for alumni, and a swimming pool.

A view of the Catherine Street Hospitals around 1925, before replacement by University Hospital. The large building in the foreground is the Psychopathic Hospital, while just behind it is the Surgical Ward (formerly Allopathic Hospital). At the time this photograph was taken, the United States medical community recognized the Catherine Street Hospitals as the largest teaching hospital in the nation.

A picture of University Hospital taken from the Medical School in 1925. Also known as Old Main, the building was open for use in August 1925. Constructed in the shape of a double Y, University Hospital boasted ten acres of floor space and two miles of corridors. In 1931, two additional stories were added.

The former Cincinnati Reds and New York Yankees pitcher Ray Fisher was baseball coach for the Wolverines for 38 years, from 1921 until 1958. He is shown here in 1925. During his tenure, the Wolverines won 15 Big Ten Conference titles and one National Collegiate Athletic Association championship, in 1953. He led the team to an overall record of 637-294-8. Nineteen of his players went on to the major leagues.

By the early 1920s, the College of Literature, Science, and the Arts needed a new home, prompting construction of James B. Angell Hall, shown here October 25, 1925. Built directly in front of University Hall, Angell Hall's designer featured a classical model with eight Doric columns and a wide expanse of steps at the facade.

Coeds swim at the Michigan Union pool around 1925. The pool, along with a library on the second floor, was originally left unfinished. Alumni and students eventually found funding for the $40,000 needed to complete the pool. At this time, women were only allowed to enter the Union in the presence of a male escort and only through the North entrance.

The Freshman-Sophomore Tug-of-War across the Huron River during the Spring Games of 1926 drew a crowd to the banks of the river. A popular place for the tug-of-war was the span of the Huron River near the Wall Street Bridge.

Philip Northrup, shown doing the long jump in 1927, was the individual NCAA champ in javelin (1925, 1926) and pole vault (1925). The coach of the track team during Northrup's time at the university was Stephen Farrell.

The Thomas Henry Simpson Memorial Institute of Medical Research is shown as it stood in 1927. The building was completed in 1926. The Institute was a gift from Mrs. Christine McDonald Simpson in memory of her husband, Thomas Henry Simpson, who had died of pernicious anemia. The building was constructed with the stipulation that it be used to investigate all aspects of pernicious anemia and help those afflicted with it.

A group of students roller skates in front of Angell Hall in 1927. During this time, student-owned automobiles were banned on campus, except for extraordinary circumstances. At one point, it is said that students decided to retaliate against the administration and turned the Diag into a roller rink.

The William L. Clements Library in 1927. Built in 1923 on South University Avenue next to the president's house, one of the original professors' houses had to be demolished to make room for it. When constructed, the West Physics Building stood to the north. The library was originally built to hold a rare book collection donated to the university by William L. Clements of Bay City, Michigan. The building still stands today.

A group of women practice archery in the late 1920s. The sport did not become a part of the Michigan Intercollegiate Athletic Association until 1952.

In 1926, the Alumni Residence at 1219 Washtenaw Avenue was purchased by the university to be used as a dormitory for women. Shown here in 1928, the building was the former residence of William D. Harriman. In 1944, the name was changed to Mary Markley House, in honor of Mary Elizabeth Butler Markley, one of the first women to graduate from UM. The building closed in 1950.

The Alexander G. Ruthven Museums Building was built when the need for natural history museum space exceeded what was available. Constructed in 1928, around the time this photograph was taken, the building housed the museums of anthropology, zoology, and paleontology and the University Herbarium. The main entrance, with its doors of perforated bronze, was at the corner of North University and Washtenaw avenues. Museum Director Ruthven was also the seventh president of the university.

A football game against Harvard University at Michigan Stadium, November 9, 1929. The Wolverines won 14–12 in front of 85,042 spectators.

Jean Paul Slusser, an instructor and graduate of the university, holds an art class in the Law Quadrangle around 1930.

Located east of the Women's Athletic Field on Observatory Street, Mosher-Jordan Halls was the first large women's dormitory at the University of Michigan. It was completed in the summer of 1930. With a capacity of 450, the building was actually two residence halls joined by a kitchen. Its name honors the first two deans of women, Eliza M. Mosher and Myra B. Jordan.

Drake's Sandwich Shop faced the Diag on North University, and attracted all sorts of people, from townies to students to the Ann Arbor Police Force. In this photograph from the 1930s, signs in the windows advertise Ice Cold Buttermilk for 10¢ and Fresh Lemonade for 15¢. The shop closed in 1993.

Students enjoy a sunny stroll through campus around 1930.

Track star Eddie Tolan crossing the 200-meter-dash finish line and setting an Olympic record. Tolan competed for UM from 1929 to 1931 and set numerous records in sprinting. At the 1932 Los Angeles Olympics, Tolan became the first African-American to win two gold medals, setting Olympic records in both the 100-meter and 200-meter dashes.

West Engineering Building and the Denison Archway, 1921. The original plans for the West Engineering Building, designed by architects Kahn and Mason, would have blocked the diagonal walkway. Engineering Professor Charles Simeon Denison drew the arch sketch that provided the solution for the blocked path.

Students walking through the Diag around 1937. The style of dress at this time was much more formal than in later years.

One of the last Senior Swing Outs before the custom ended in 1934.

Female students in a "correctives class" in Barbour Gymnasium, 1937. A well-equipped corrective room was a part of the gymnasium, and allowed for women with temporary or permanent disabilities to participate in physical education.

Construction of the Horace H. Rackham School of Graduate Studies in 1937. The trustees of the Horace H. Rackham and Mary A. Rackham Fund gave the building, along with a generous endowment, to the university. The building was dedicated in June 1938.

Paul Kromer (no. 83) opens a hole for his "Touchdown Twin" Tom Harmon (no. 98) in their 14–0 victory over Illinois in 1938. Kromer and Harmon sport the winged helmet design, which debuted that season at the opener against Michigan State. Coach Herbert O. "Fritz" Crisler had the design painted on the helmet in maize and blue. The design has come to represent University of Michigan football, although other Michigan teams have adopted the pattern as well.

Bill Watson vaults over the high jump for the track team in the late 1930s. Known as "Big Bill," he was the first black athlete to be elected captain of the Michigan track team. The Wolverines won Big Ten team championships each year of Watson's tenure, when he was also the individual winner of the long jump. He was inducted into the UM Hall of Honor posthumously in 1982.

Bennie Oosterbaan received the Western Conference Medal for both academic and athletic excellence and was honored as an All-American five times while playing for Michigan: three times for football (1925, 1926, 1927) and twice for basketball (1927, 1928). In 1928, he led the basketball conference in scoring with 178 points. Oosterbaan also served as basketball coach from 1939 to 1946 and coached the Wolverine football team from 1948 to 1958. He was Coach of the Year in 1948, when his team shared the National Championship with Notre Dame.

Wartime Advances in Science and Law

(1940–1949)

A boy peers through the gate to Ferry Field. Albert Kahn designed the gate and surrounding brick wall containing ticket windows. Dexter M. Ferry, Detroit businessman and philanthropist, gave the university 20 acres for athletic use and funds for the gate.

Stockwell Hall around 1940. Set on the Hill, this all-female dormitory overlooked Palmer Field, the women's physical education grounds. Stockwell Hall was named after Madelon Louisa Stockwell, the first woman admitted to the university, in 1870. Stockwell Hall remains an all-female residence.

Director of University Museums Dr. Carl E. Guthe sits on a Greenfield Village horse-drawn bus with a driver in this 1941 photograph.

Members of the Ski Club enjoy a wintry day in Michigan as they pose near the bus during the 1940s.

Interior view of the Sports Coliseum in 1940, depicting its structure made of concrete and steel. Located at the corner of Hill Street and Fifth Avenue, the coliseum was used as a skating rink and for ice hockey.

View down Ingalls Mall of Rackham Graduate School and Burton Tower, around 1940. The Mall bridges the distance between Rackham and the Graduate Library.

Football legend Tom Harmon and actress Anita Louise, his costar in *Harmon of Michigan*, pose next to the Michigan League's "Sunday Morning" fountain in 1941.

Students take a break to enjoy the Michigan winter weather during wartime.

Women help in the war effort by selling defense bonds on campus, 1942.

Early morning sunlight streams through the trees as students walk through the Diag in 1947.

The 1948 UM hockey team, led by coach Vic Heyliger, won the first NCAA Championship Tournament with an 8–4 victory over Dartmouth. Coach Heyliger won a record six national titles and was inducted into the U.S. Hockey Hall of Fame and the University of Michigan Hall of Honor. His UM teams established a 228-61-13 record between 1944 and 1957.

A drawing class in the College of Architecture and Design, 1949.

Architecture and design class in the Lorch Hall sculpture garden around 1949.

Students filing into the stands on Ferry Field, June 11, 1949, for commencement. Both University Hall and Hill Auditorium had previously served as sites for commencement exercises.

North University, near State Street, is the site of Hill Auditorium. The building was constructed in 1913 in order to allow the campus adequate space for convocations and performances. The construction was funded largely by Regent Arthur Hill, in whose honor the building is named. Despite its large size, Hill Auditorium is known for excellent acoustics. Burton Memorial Tower is in the background.

Changing Times and Building New Resources

(1950–1970s)

Observatory at Portage Lake. The building of the University Hospital and increasing city lights in Ann Arbor caused the Detroit Observatory to be ineffective. Two hundred acres at Portage Lake, about 15 miles outside the city, were acquired for new telescopes.

McMath-Hulbert Observatory, located at Lake Angelus (near Pontiac) was founded by businessman Francis C. McMath, his son Robert R. McMath, and Judge Henry S. Hulbert. Director of the Astronomy Department, Ralph H. Curtiss, became interested when he saw moving pictures of the moon taken at the observatory in 1928. The property was deeded to the university in 1939.

Harlan Hatcher (UM President), Walker Cisler (President, Detroit Edison Company), Dean Sawyer (Dean of Rackham and the Director of the Michigan Memorial Phoenix Project), Chester Lang (VP, General Electric), and George Romney (President, American Motors Corporation and later governor) were among those present for the Phoenix Project Memorial Laboratory dedication on Atom Day, June 9, 1955. The laboratory is a working memorial to University members who lost their lives in World War II and is dedicated to developing peaceful uses for nuclear technology.

Students congregate on the steps of Angell Hall between 1951 and 1960. This photo shows the Doric columns and wide expanse of steps chosen by the architect, Albert Kahn. Around this time, new auditoriums for Angell Hall were under construction.

Michigan Stadium aerial view, around 1950. The old wooden bleachers were replaced with steel ones shortly before this picture was taken. The additional seating boosted attendance to 97,239 people from 85,753.

Students stand outside the Waterman gym for registration and orientation in September 1951.

Fiftieth Reunion, Class of 1903.

All-American Robert White, hockey team, 1958–1960. White helped win the bronze medal for Canada at the 1956 Olympics in Cortina, Italy.

The announcement of the polio vaccine on April 12, 1955, by President Harlan Hatcher, Professor Thomas Francis, Jonas Salk, and Basil O'Connor (friend and law partner to President Franklin Roosevelt). While Salk attended the University of Michigan to study virology, Thomas Francis taught him vaccine development. After UM he worked at the University of Pittsburgh and the National Foundation for Infantile Paralysis. UM was the largest grant recipient of the foundation.

A view of the gallery in the Martha Cook Dormitory around 1960. Its Gothic and Renaissance style makes this building one of the most striking on campus. The corridor has a floor of marble and red flagged paving, with oak paneled walls. At the end of the gallery is a replica of the statue of the Venus de Milo.

John F. Kennedy proposes the Peace Corps on the Michigan Union steps at 2:00 A.M., October 14, 1960. Then-Senator Kennedy began this unprepared speech by saying, "I want to express my thanks to you, as a graduate of the Michigan of the East, Harvard University." He continued the speech by challenging students to commit to several years of public service.

The Cube, shown here, around 1968. Located in Regents Plaza, this gift from the Class of 1965 spins on its axis when you push it. The Cube's designer, Tony Rosenthal, was a graduate of the class of 1936. Campus legend says that the president gives it a ceremonial push each morning on the way to his office in order to get the university under way.

University graduate Maxine (Micki) King shown with her gold medal from the 1972 Munich Olympic Games. She won the gold medal in the three-meter dive and placed fifth in platform diving. While at Michigan, King was twice All-American goalie for the water polo team. She went on to coach at the United States Military Academy.

Gerald Ford stands with Coach Bo Schembechler at football practice in 1972. Ford's football jersey, number 48, was retired at the October 1994 Michigan State game. Schembechler was UM's winningest head coach (1967–1989), with a 194-48-5 record, and served as director of athletics, 1988–1990.

Notes on the Photographs

These notes, listed by page number, attempt to include all aspects known of the photographs. Each of the photographs is identified by the page number, a title or description, photographer and collection, archive, and call or box number when applicable. Although every attempt was made to collect all data, in some cases complete data may have been unavailable due to the age and condition of some of the photographs and records.

II **MICHIGAN FOOTBALL**
Bentley Historical Library, University of Michigan
BL001068

VI **A BLOCK M**
Bentley Historical Library, University of Michigan
9622 Aa2

VIII **MICHIGAN THEATER**
Bentley Historical Library, University of Michigan
BL005321

X **MASON HALL**
Bentley Historical Library, University of Michigan
BL004476

2 **MEMORIAL BOULDER**
Bentley Historical Library, University of Michigan
BL004485

3 **LAW BUILDING**
Bentley Historical Library, University of Michigan
BL000278

4 **WALKWAY TO CLASS**
Bentley Historical Library, University of Michigan
BL001936

5 **UNIVERSITY HALL**
Bentley Historical Library, University of Michigan
BL004534

6 **CHEMICAL LAB**
Bentley Historical Library, University of Michigan
BL004165

7 **READING IN THE GRASS**
Bentley Historical Library, University of Michigan
BL004533

8 **LAW LIBRARY**
Bentley Historical Library, University of Michigan
BL000065

9 **CREW TEAM ON HURON**
Bentley Historical Library, University of Michigan
BL003684

10 **LAW BUILDING**
Bentley Historical Library, University of Michigan
BL003514

11 **FOOTBALL TEAM**
Bentley Historical Library, University of Michigan
BL001001

12 **THE DIAG**
Bentley Historical Library, University of Michigan
BL001875

13 **UNIVERSITY HALL, 1880**
Bentley Historical Library, University of Michigan
BL004527

14 **CREW TEAM ON HURON**
Bentley Historical Library, University of Michigan
BL003684

15 **LAW BUILDING**
Bentley Historical Library, University of Michigan
BL003514

16 **FOOTBALL TEAM**
Bentley Historical Library, University of Michigan
BL001001

17 **THE DIAG**
Bentley Historical Library, University of Michigan
BL001875

18 **UNIVERSITY HALL, 1880**
Bentley Historical Library, University of Michigan
BL004527

14 **ENGINEERING BUILDING**
Bentley Historical Library, University of Michigan
BL000104

15 **CHEQUAMEGON BAND**
Bentley Historical Library, University of Michigan
BL000380

16 **JOHN JACOB ABEL**
Bentley Historical Library, University of Michigan
BL002050

17 **UM HOSPITAL**
Bentley Historical Library, University of Michigan
BL001740

18 **MEDICAL BUILDING**
Bentley Historical Library, University of Michigan
BL005294

19 **NEWBERRY HALL**
Bentley Historical Library, University of Michigan
BL005112

20 **1891 FOOTBALL TEAM**
Bentley Historical Library, University of Michigan
BL000944

21 **ANATOMICAL LABORATORY**
Bentley Historical Library, University of Michigan
BL002089

22 **DISSECTING ROOM**
Bentley Historical Library, University of Michigan
BL002091

23 **STATE STREET**
Bentley Historical Library, University of Michigan
BL001941

24 **ALICE HAMILTON**
Bentley Historical Library, University of Michigan
BL002078

70 **Yost Field House**
Bentley Historical Library, University of Michigan
BL004671

71 **Exterior of Field House**
Bentley Historical Library, University of Michigan
BL004674

72 **Marine Band**
Bentley Historical Library, University of Michigan
BL003655

73 **Michigan Union**
Bentley Historical Library, University of Michigan
BL004719

74 **Catherine Street**
Bentley Historical Library, University of Michigan
BL005107

75 **University Hospital**
Bentley Historical Library, University of Michigan
BL001827

76 **Ray Fisher**
Bentley Historical Library, University of Michigan
BL001090

77 **College of Literature**
Bentley Historical Library, University of Michigan
BL001967

78 **Swimming Pool**
Bentley Historical Library, University of Michigan
BL001143

79 **Tug-of-War**
Bentley Historical Library, University of Michigan
BL003706

80 **Philip Northrup**
Bentley Historical Library, University of Michigan
BL001110

81 **Research Building**
Bentley Historical Library, University of Michigan
BL004475

82 **Roller Skating**
Bentley Historical Library, University of Michigan
BL000004

83 **Clements Library, 1927**
Bentley Historical Library, University of Michigan
BL004657

84 **Archers**
Bentley Historical Library, University of Michigan
BL003678

85 **Alumni Residence**
Bentley Historical Library, University of Michigan
BL001778

86 **Museums Building**
Bentley Historical Library, University of Michigan
BL001770

87 **Game at Michigan Stadium**
Bentley Historical Library, University of Michigan
BL000081

88 **Jean Paul Slusser**
Bentley Historical Library, University of Michigan
BL000002

89 **Mosher-Jordan Halls**
Bentley Historical Library, University of Michigan
BL001668

90 **Sandwich Shop**
Bentley Historical Library, University of Michigan
BL005318

91 **Sunny Stroll**
Bentley Historical Library, University of Michigan
BL003812

92 **Eddie Tolan**
Bentley Historical Library, University of Michigan
BL001105

93 **Denison Archway**
Bentley Historical Library, University of Michigan
BL004628

94 **The Diag**
Bentley Historical Library, University of Michigan
BL001866

95 **Senior Swing Out**
Bentley Historical Library, University of Michigan
BL003806

96 **Correctives Class**
Bentley Historical Library, University of Michigan
BL000268

97 **Construction**
Bentley Historical Library, University of Michigan
BL004391

98 **"Touchdown Twins"**
Bentley Historical Library, University of Michigan
BL001066

99 **Bill Watson**
Bentley Historical Library, University of Michigan
BL001106

100 **Bennie Oosterbaan**
Bentley Historical Library, University of Michigan
BL008383

102 **Gate to Ferry Field**
Bentley Historical Library, University of Michigan
BL003809

103 **Stockwell Hall**
Bentley Historical Library, University of Michigan
BL004505

104 **Horse-Drawn Bus**
Bentley Historical Library, University of Michigan
BL006415

105 **Ski Club**
Bentley Historical Library, University of Michigan
BL003807

106 **Sports Coliseum**
Bentley Historical Library, University of Michigan
BL004107

107 **Burton Tower, 1940**
Bentley Historical Library, University of Michigan
BL004060

108 **Sunday Morning Fountain**
Bentley Historical Library, University of Michigan
BL001078

109 **Snowball Fight**
Bentley Historical Library, University of Michigan
BL003723

110 **Selling War Bonds**
Bentley Historical Library, University of Michigan
BL005309

111 **Diag in Early Morning**
Bentley Historical Library, University of Michigan
BL000243

112 **UM Hockey Team**
Bentley Historical Library, University of Michigan
BL003076

113 **Drawing Class**
Bentley Historical Library, University of Michigan
BL000246

114 **SCULPTURE GARDEN CLASS**
Bentley Historical Library, University of Michigan
BL005241

115 **COMMENCEMENT, 1949**
Bentley Historical Library, University of Michigan
BL000240

116 **HILL AUDITORIUM**
Bentley Historical Library, University of Michigan
BL005046

118 **OBSERVATORY**
Bentley Historical Library, University of Michigan
BL001701

119 **OBSERVATORY NO. 2**
Bentley Historical Library, University of Michigan
BL005250

120 **ATOM DAY DEDICATION**
Bentley Historical Library, University of Michigan
HS1818

121 **ANGELL HALL**
Bentley Historical Library, University of Michigan
BL001798

122 **MICHIGAN STADIUM**
Bentley Historical Library, University of Michigan
BL004766175

123 **REGISTRATION**
Bentley Historical Library, University of Michigan
BL000236

124 **FIFTIETH REUNION**
Bentley Historical Library, University of Michigan
BL003656

125 **ROBERT WHITE**
Bentley Historical Library, University of Michigan
BL003245

126 **POLIO VACCINE**
Bentley Historical Library, University of Michigan
BL006836

127 **MARTHA COOK DORM**
Bentley Historical Library, University of Michigan
BL000062185

128 **JFK**
Bentley Historical Library, University of Michigan
BL000107

129 **THE CUBE**
Bentley Historical Library, University of Michigan
BL004498

130 **MAXINE "MICKI" KING**
Bentley Historical Library, University of Michigan
BL001145

131 **FORD AND SCHEMBECHLER**
Bentley Historical Library, University of Michigan
BL003031

CPSIA information can be obtained
at www.ICGtesting.com
Printed in the USA
JSHW041216140323
38933JS00003B/8

9 781683 368939